STOLEN VOICES

Nativida Etienne-Maule

The internet addresses, email addresses and phone numbers in this book are accurate at the time of publication, They are provided as a resource.

"To all the mothers who donated ultrasound pictures:

Thank you for allowing your beautiful children to help save millions of babies from being slaughtered in the womb. May God raise these little warriors to be as bold and mighty in the fight against abortion. God bless you and your families."

stolenvoices18@gmail.com

DEDICATION

I dedicate this book to my loving children, Tyreek, Tiyana, Tanaya, and Nigel JR. You are my gifts from God that keep me going in life. I thank God for you every day.

This book is written for the preborn that never took their first breath or shared their voices to speak or cry. May you sleep in the everlasting arms of our Savior.

Finally, I dedicate this book to you, the reader. May you hear God's voice as you digest every word in this book. Also, may it bring healing, awareness, and closure. For those of you wrestling with the decision to give your child life, may the Lord speak to you through this book.

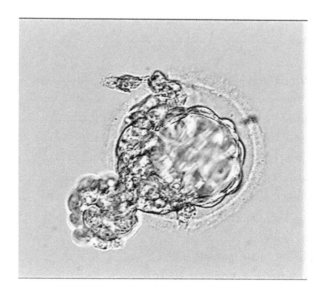

Life Begins At Conception

"Before I formed you in your mother's womb I chose you. Before you were born I set you apart."

Jeremiah 1:5 NET

TABLE OF CONTENTS

INTRODUCTION

In 2008, after watching an abortion on television, I heard God crying out for all the children that were killed by abortion. After watching the baby in the womb being torn and ripped apart to pieces, God began to remind me of my past abortions. He told me that I must speak for the babies that had their lives stolen from abortion's deadly sting. I was directed and commissioned by the Lord to speak for the children that have died, the ones that live, and the ones that are yet to come.

I pray and hope that after reading my personal experience as a post-abortive woman, your hearts will change and many will receive healing from the stain abortion has left in the innermost parts of our hearts.

I am speaking to the woman who is thinking about getting an abortion and the woman who has already had an abortion; you are not alone. I found myself in your positions and I cannot say that it is an easy place to be in.

Although I have had several abortions, I am not proud of my past decisions. I had my first abortion at the age of fourteen. My family, who thought they were making the right decision for me, took me to have this abortion. I never told the father because I was afraid and confused. This experience was one of the most traumatic and terrifying experiences of my life. I found myself partially sedated, lying on a cold table at the private office of an abortionist. This person never asked me any questions and did not take into consideration that I was a scared little girl. The procedure was never explained to me and I remember crying throughout the whole process. I remember feeling pressure in my pelvic area and heard suctioning in the background.

At that very moment of my first abortion, I did not know I was killing a part of me that day my baby was removed from me. That day opened doors for future abortions in my life. My baby deserved a chance to live and I didn't have the voice or strength to fight for his or her life. After I had this abortion, my family never spoke about it again. I tucked this little secret deep in my heart and thought it would not resurface again.

I tried to forget this horrific day, but God reminded me when I got saved that I took a precious life that He created. God brought this abortion and the ones after this to my remembrance.

At sixteen years old, I found myself pregnant again and my son's father tried to pressure me into getting an abortion. However, I stood my ground and didn't give in to his request to terminate the baby. I was going to keep my baby despite my age and what others said about me. I was told by naysayers that I was going to drop out of high school, end up homeless, and become unsuccessful in life. Fortunately, my family was very supportive this time and I was able to keep my baby while finishing high school.   My son's father was a very abusive man who took advantage of the fact that I was much younger than him and he tried to control and manipulate me. After my son was born, the physical and mental abuse I received from him became worse. I was constantly on edge because anything could trigger an argument or physical altercation.

I found myself pregnant for him twice at the age of 17—both pregnancies resulted in an abortion. I was scared to leave him because he always threatened to hurt me if I did. I never told my family I was pregnant because I was afraid of their judgment. At the time, I thought I was doing what was best for *my* life by taking away my children's lives.

I went on to graduate from high school at the age of seventeen. I started college that year and was able to find the courage to leave my son's father.

Following that relationship, I had one last abortion before I realized that what I was doing was wrong. This abortion was the turning point in my life, which changed my destructive behavior.

At twenty-one, I found myself pregnant after graduating from college and working in the medical field.

I fell in love with a man who said all the right things and told me everything I wanted to hear. He promised to marry me and sold me a fairytale dream of happily ever after until I found out I was pregnant. I wanted to keep my baby, but he pressured me into another abortion. I remember the hurt I felt at the abortion clinic. He was there with me and promised me everything was going to be alright and that we would get married soon. After going through the abortion, I felt empty and disappointed with myself. I tried to call him the next day but I got no answer. This man who promised me that I would be his wife abandoned me after pressuring me into killing his child. I felt used and stupid for believing him. I fell into a deep state of depression and would cry at all times. I lost a substantial amount of weight and suffered from loss of appetite. All through this tough time, I never told my family about the hurt I was feeling. At that time, I did not have a real relationship with the Lord, but I made a promise that I would never abort another child of mine again.

When I gave my life to Christ in 2006, He reminded me of the lives that I sacrificed upon the altar of convenience. I cried and wept before God and asked Him to forgive me. That very day, I felt a burden lifted off of me. Jesus forgave me for my past abortions! He gave me a new beginning and created a new heart in me as the Psalmist says in Psalm 51!

I want to tell the woman that is contemplating abortion that even though it may seem like the best decision for you right now, one day, you will think back on this decision and may regret it. Remember, the enemy comes to kill, steal, and destroy, but our Lord and Savior, Jesus, came to give life and redemption! Whatever the circumstances, God has a plan for your child!

I destroyed the lives of my babies because I thought I was doing what was best for me at that time. Even though I had many obstacles to overcome and was a teenage mom, I was able to graduate from high school at the age of seventeen. I also found the strength and courage to break away from an abusive and toxic relationship. You can do it too!

I was able to graduate from college and now hold professional degrees as a health care provider. I was given the grace to conceive again and have four wonderful children, as well as a wonderful husband who loves and supports me. I could have never accomplished these things if God did not heal and deliver me from my past sins.

To all my beautiful sisters, there is hope for you and your babies. Trust me, I was in your place several years ago, and I can truthfully say that you don't need to have an abortion to achieve your goals.

I declare that you can be a mother and still finish school, have a career, and find the right man who will love you for you someday. Remember, any man that loves will never pressure you into killing your child because real men protect and love their families.

Abortion is a lie from the enemy who is seeking to devour the baby in your womb. Choose life for your baby! There are many resources available that will help you during and after pregnancy. Before making a hasty decision, find a pregnancy center, or get an ultrasound so that you can see your baby and hear his or her tiny heartbeat. This baby is your baby, and you are his or her mother. The life growing inside your womb is a person that was purposed to live a life beyond the womb. God *will* provide! If he took care of me and my children, trust me, He will do it for you!

For the woman who has already had an abortion(s), Jesus says He forgives you. Go and sin no more! The scripture made it clear that there is no condemnation for those who are in Christ Jesus. Once you have repented of your sins and past abortion, your judgment is gone! Take comfort that one day you will see your baby in heaven. Your baby loves you and so does the Lord. Be healed today from the pain, hurt, rejection, depression, oppression, anxiety, condemnation, and impoverished spirit.

I pray for God to open doors that no man can shut! I speak healing and life in your wombs! I declare that the barren wombs will be fruitful and multiply again! I pray that God will bless you and make you mothers of many generations to come! I declare and decree that the fruit of the womb will be your reward!

We break every generational curse that is upon your lives! We break the curse of poverty, abortion, and addiction, and I speak the peace of God upon you! May the peace that surpasses all understanding guard your hearts and minds! I pray this book will bless everyone that reads it!

I pray that you will hear the cry of the *stolen voices* of the babies who were killed and are currently at risk of death by abortion's deadly sting.

They are pleading with humanity; please let them live!

I began writing this book in 2008, right after the Holy Spirit prompted me to watch an abortion on television. After watching the abortion, I received a heavy burden in my heart for the preborn.

This book was written to give preborn children a voice, so that others may hear their cry to live. It was also written to bring healing to those who have had abortions for various reasons.

This book recognizes that abortion is not an easy choice to make for some women and that many have had an abortion for varying reasons. Since 1973, when the Supreme Court first handed down its decision in Roe v Wade, there have been approximately 60 million babies aborted. These are 60 million children that God knew and knitted in His image for His purpose and glory. Today, we are facing a crisis in the United States. Many laws have been erected and even more are being proposed to abort babies until their birth. My prayer is for the body of Christ to take a stand and become a voice for preborn and born children alike. The Bible tells us that we must open our mouths on behalf of those unable to speak for the legal rights of all the dying (Proverbs 31:8).

I pray that this book blesses you and brings healing and redemption to your soul. For all the women who have had abortions, remember that God loves you and is extending healing and forgiveness to you, even at this moment. The Word of God says that there is no condemnation for those who are in Christ Jesus. Whom the Lord has set free is free indeed. Forgive yourself as God has forgiven you today. I want you to put your hand on your heart and pray these words: "Father, in the name of Jesus, I curse the trauma caused by the grief and loss from my past abortion(s). I curse the spirit of trauma and the spirit of grief, and I break their power over me, in Jesus' name.

I pray for joy to be restored in my heart to strengthen me.

Thank you, Lord, for forgiving me as I forgive myself. I close every door where I have allowed sin to enter my life through abortion(s). I declare that I am free today. I pray this in Jesus' name. Amen."

PART ONE:

HEAR MY CRY TO LIVE

Stolen Voices

Lord, society says abortion is a woman's choice;

what happens to the little stolen voice?

Who will cry out for them and who will lament for they've lost their lives without consent.

"My dearest mother, if only you knew how much I love and have truly missed you. I will never know and see your beautiful face.

My life was taken, and now it is too late.

I've met a friend who has taken me up in his loving hands.

The day I was forsaken and aborted from His divine plan.

I will never cry for my voice was prematurely stolen;

I was left torn in pieces, for my bones have been broken.

I will always live in your heart, remember my still voice

for I have lost my life without a choice."

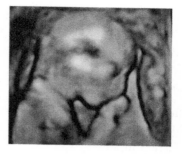

Open your mouth on behalf of those unable to speak, for the legal rights of all the dying.

Proverbs 31:8 NET

I Live Inside

Does my mother know that I'm alive because, in the womb, I quietly hide.

It's still early for me to be detected because I am growing secretly inside

Did you know that blood contains life and power?

That I am growing and changing every second of the hour

The wisdom of this world is foolish to the One who've created me

Some people believe in the things they can only touch and see

I am living inside my mother's womb, can you see my tiny heart beating strong?

Why are so many babies aborted daily when my Creator says it is wrong?

Why are they trying to take my life away based on theories and lies?

Can they not hear my tiny cries?

Why I'm being silenced, and they're trying to steal my voice.

When I lay here helplessly unable to make a choice.

Society says that my mother has the power and right to choose.

I cannot fight for my life, am I the one that must lose.

My beloved mother, before you make this important choice and decision;

Look closely at the ultrasound screen and see that there is life growing inside, perfectly hidden.

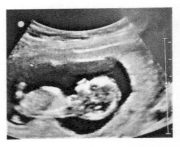

My bones were not hidden from you when I was being made in secret, when I was skillfully woven in an underground workshop.

Psalm 139:15 GW

Pray and ask God

Do you need evidence to see so that you may believe that I have a soul from the moment I was conceived?

Do you need confirmation for you to realize and know?

That I exist and live, and my heart pumps and blood flows,

What will it take for you to truly understand?

That when you take my life away, you will abort God's divine plan.

Would you have known my fate and my destiny?

That I could have been the one who discovered the cure for cancer or HIV

If you are still struggling with the decision of what to do with me

Pray and ask God who I will grow up to be,

Before I am aborted and left to die alone and cold.

Pray and ask God if I really have a soul

I am not speaking on this matter to induce your guilt and shame.

Please pray and ask God, for He has chosen my name.

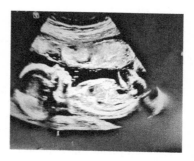

The Lord called me from the womb, from the body of my mother He named me.

Isaiah 49:1 ESV

Your eyes saw me when I was only a fetus. Every day [of my life] was recorded in your book before one of them had taken place.

Psalm 139:16 GW

I Shall not Die

I shall not die but live to declare the Lord's work and plan.

I am fearfully and wonderfully made, the splendid work of His loving hand.

If you can hear my voice, then I am still here with you.

You have chosen to give me back my life and have allowed God's plan to go through.

Thank you for making the right and correct choice.

I praise God that the enemy did not have a chance to steal my voice.

My mother and father, you will not regret this life-changing decision.

You have allowed God's plan for good to prevail and thwarted the enemy's destructive mission.

The Blood of the Lamb has overcome abortion, and now I will live and not die.

Satan has been defeated, and we have exposed his deception and lies.

Now that my voice has been restored, I can speak boldly and free.

So, I can cry out for another baby's life in this world just like you have done for me.

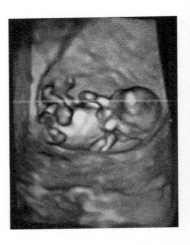

I will not die, but live, and I will proclaim what the LORD has done.

Psalms 118:17 NET

I am God's Beloved

How will I ever live my life if it is suddenly taken away?

Will I ever be able to use my lips to sing, praise, and pray?

If my body loses its precious feet and soft little hands,

How will I ever be able to clap and playfully jump and dance?

If my body is ripped into pieces and my organs are taken apart,

Will I ever get to love you unconditionally if I am left without a heart?

How will I ever think and reason if my brain is suctioned out of my head?

Will I ever get to comprehend and enjoy a bedtime story that was read?

If I was created to be a part of the Kingdom of our Lord,

Will you still abort me If I am His beloved?

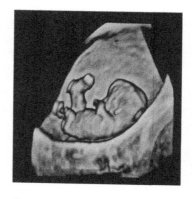

Your eyes saw me when I was only a fetus. Every day [of my life] was recorded in your book before one of them had taken place.

Psalm 139:16 GW

Beautifully Created

Rape, mental retardation, birth defects, did God make a mistake?

When a baby is not what you expected to be, will you still take his or her life away?

Are they not fearfully and wonderfully made by God's sovereign hands?

Who are we to decide who is part of his divine plan?

The Lord has a plan for the child with birth and chromosomal defects.

Beautifully created, His chosen and elect,

Who are we to decide who lives or dies on this earth?

Every life the Lord created deserves their special birth.

God knew exactly how he formed us all to be.

Ask the Lord to give you His sight and behold what He marvelously sees,

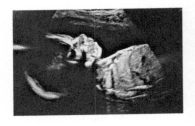

I will give thanks to you because I have been so amazingly and miraculously made.

Your works are miraculous, and my soul is fully aware of this.

Psalm 139:14 GW

Will You Ever Know?

Will I ever be given a chance by my beloved mother to see your beautiful face?

Will I ever look into your eyes and see who held my fate?

Will I ever be given a chance for you to hear my cries?

Will I have to bear death's sting that will leave me to die?

Will I learn to say my first words and call out your lovely name?

Will my life end now with sorrow and pain?

Will I learn to live in God's peace and serenity?

Will I be given a chance to grow into who I am purposed to be?

Will I ever take my very first breath?

Will you allow the enemy to kill another one of God's elect?

Will I ever know? That is a good question to ask?

Only you know the answers will you please respond to that?

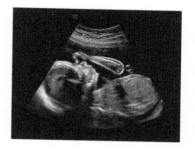

God's Spirit has made me. The breath of the Almighty gives me life.

Job 33:4 GW

My First Selfie

Look at the ultrasound screen closely, and I will show you something great.

Look closely at my features and my sweet and lovely face.

I am a miracle and an unsolved mystery.

The wise men of this world are constantly trying to prove my viability.

They cannot understand how the Almighty God keeps me alive.

They continue to seek knowledge, but the Lord confounds the wise.

If you are confused about what to believe, just take a closer look at me.

Look at the ultrasound screen and see my very first selfie.

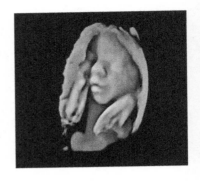

But God, who appointed me before I was born and who called me by his kindness, was pleased.

Galatians 1:15 GW

Abortion Stops a Beating Heart

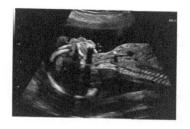

Abortion stops a beating heart.

A heart that was designed to be set apart.

Abortion stops a heart filled with hopeful beats.

A rhythm that was terminated when the heart sound ceased.

Abortion stops a beating heart that was created to live with purpose and determination.

Will this beat stop in the womb that was designed for its refuge and protection?

Abortion stops a beating heart that the Lord divinely knitted with His hands.

Will you allow another heartbeat to stop because of the enemy's evil plans?

The thief comes only to steal and kill and destroy; I have come so that they may have life and may have it abundantly.

John 10:10 NET

My 6 Month Growth

My growth remains a scientific mystery,

Only those who have God's eyes can truly see life in me.

Do you know what happens at the end of my fourth week?

My tiny heart is pumping at 65 minutes per beat.

At six weeks, a beautiful heart rhythm can be detected and found.

You can see the image of my heart beating on the screen of the ultrasound.

At 12 weeks, I have two arms, legs, feet, and all my tiny fingers and toes

Surprise, I'm a girl or boy, too soon for the ultrasound to show.

I am 16 weeks, and my heartbeat is audible through a doppler instrument.

Now, when you look at me on the ultrasound screen, you can tell my sex and facial development.

I'm 15 weeks, and my legs are moving fast and quick.

You can finally feel me giving you a strong and powerful kick.

I'm 20 weeks, and I can physically respond to light, sound, and the touch of your soft hands.

I can express the painful and hurtful pangs.

I am 24 weeks, my lungs are maturing, and I can live outside my mother's body with artificial support.

Did you know my life began at conception, will you believe the enemy's lies or the Lord's truthful report?

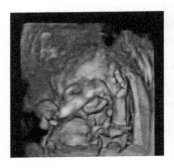

You alone created my inner being. You knitted me together inside my mother.

Psalm 139:14 GW

Chance to Live

From my mother's womb, I was removed and killed.

My remains were thrown away, and my ashes dispersed in the hills.

Did you ever wonder where I came from or why was I sent?

Will anyone know I was gone? Will they cry for me and lament?

Was I ever real to you if no one ever touched my skin?

Will I be erased from your memories, too, as I was removed from within?

Do you know what happened to me when my life ended before the time of my birth?

My body was martyred so brutally as I became one with the earth.

Why was my life taken away? Wasn't I the Lord's precious gift?

Why didn't you give me a chance to make it and live?

If you are contemplating of having an abortion, please remember my voice.

Please give your baby a chance to live and don't allow another life to be lost.

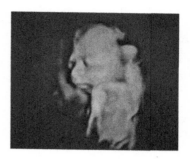

From my mother's womb, you have been my God.

Psalm 22:10 GW

Trust in What You Cannot See

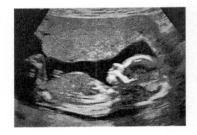

The mystery of my birth is foolish to those who possess the wisdom of this world.

The Lord has this knowledge hidden like the rarest pearl.

Scholars perform studies and reviews, trying to uncover how God knitted something so marvelous and blessed.

They will never be able to figure my development with manmade theories and tests.

Only those who have God's eyes to see can trust in the things not shown.

If you believe that I have life in me, then you will believe in the Almighty God, who sits upon the throne.

Trust the LORD with all your heart, and do not rely on your own understanding.

In all your ways acknowledge him, and he will make your paths smooth.

Proverbs 3:5-6 GW

Open Your Heart To Love Me

A heart without light will never understand the ways of our Lord Jesus Christ.

For He is the way, truth, and eternal life.

If I was given life more abundantly, why am I a topic of debate?

Why will mankind abort me and will not fight for my fate?

After listening to our stories, will you change your mind about abortion and reconsider?

Will you at least get an ultrasound and see my tiny heartbeat and figure?

Pray and ask God, and He will show you what to do.

Do not allow society to tell you lies; the Lord will show you the truth.

Open your heart to love me, and in a few months, I will see your face.

I am waiting for you, sweet mommy, so that we can cuddle and play.

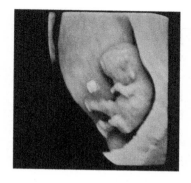

It isn't happy when injustice is done, but it is happy with the truth.

Love never stops being patient, never stops believing, never stops hoping, never gives up.

1 Corinthians 13:6-7 GW

This is Your Body, but I AM Part of You

If this is your body, why am I living inside of you?

All I want is a place to grow until the day I am due.

I can hear people saying that you have the right to choose and kill me.

How can you take my life knowing my face you will never see?

If this is your body, why do our hearts have a different beat and sound?

Please go and see my heart beating strong, mommy on the ultrasound.

I know this is your body, can I please borrow it until I am due?

So, you can learn to love me, mommy, and see that I am part of you.

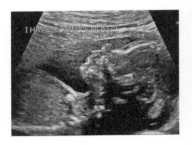

Didn't he who made me in my mother's belly make them? Didn't the same God form us in the womb?

Job 31:15 GW

Precious Reward

If you do not want me, mommy, can you find someone who will adopt me?

That is the greatest gift I can receive, and it will make me happy.

If you do not want me, mommy, can you please just let me live?

I will make some other mommy happy and our love to her, I'll give.

One day, you will know that I was a gift from the Lord.

I know you really love me, mommy, because you gave someone your precious reward.

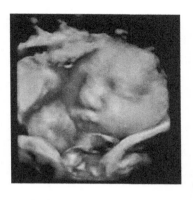

And whoever welcomes a child like this in my name welcomes me.

Matthew 18:5 GW

Ripped Apart

Help! I am being ripped apart in front of a Church located on a busy street.

They could not hear my silent cries as the doctor ripped off my feet.

No one took the time to stop my mommy as she opened the clinic door.

I heard her crying this morning as she lay confused on the floor.

If only they knew this would be my last day.

Why did they not take the time to stop by and pray?

No one remembered me as my body was ripped piece by piece.

Did they not know that I was being killed across the street?

Next time you pass by, remember this was the place where I died.

They told my mommy I was not a person and that I was not alive.

Will you stop other mommies from killing babies like me?

Will you continue to have your Church service and be blinded to what you truly see?

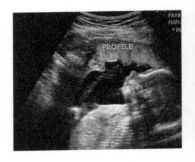

Rescue captives condemned to death, and spare those staggering toward their slaughter

Proverbs 24:11 GW

I am My Mother's Child

My mommy was beaten, raped, and cast aside.

Her heart was bruised and was left hurting inside.

She chose to give me life despite the trauma and pain.

I heard her cries because the bad man left her heart wounded and stained.

My mommy chose my life when everybody said no.

We are now healing together as my little body grows.

Mommy knew it was the bad man that injured her.

Her love grows each day for me, and we will endure this journey together.

I wished I could stop the bad man from hurting my beautiful mommy.

I know she did not deserve to be raped, and this was not caused by me.

I was created by God's merciful hands

He has a purpose for me, and I am part of His divine plan.

He never wanted a bad man to hurt my beautiful mommy.

I am the child of my mother, who unconditionally loves me.

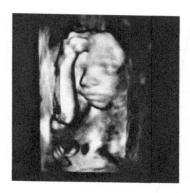

Parents must never be put to death for the crimes of their children, and children must never be put to death for the crimes of their parents. Each person must be put to death for his own crime.

Deuteronomy 24:16 GW

Mommy, You Still Hurt

Mommy, I can hear your beautiful voice singing to me.

I know you are going to love me even if my face you cannot see.

I am growing fast and strong for time seems to fly.

Every day, I can hear your heart beating, for it soothes me like a lullaby.

What happened, mommy? I feel something sharp piercing my heart.

I am starting to feel a lot of pain in my body, and it is becoming cold and dark.

Now, I am wrapped in the loving arms of a kind man who said you did not want me.

He said I am special and who I was meant to be.

He told me that if you trusted Him, that He would open a special door.

He would have taken care of both of us, so we would not have to be poor.

He sent me to you so I could be your special little girl.

We were going to do nice things together and travel the world.

Mommy, now that I am going to miss your sweet voice,

Why are you still sad and lonely? Did you make the right choice?

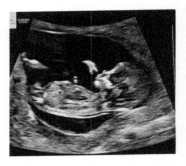

I call on heaven and earth as witnesses today that I have offered you life or death, blessings, or curses. Choose life so that you and your descendants will live.

Deuteronomy 30:19 GW

Lord Forgive My Mother and Father

Lord, forgive my mother and father, for they do not know what they do.

For they do not truly know what is required of You.

If they knew Your truth, my life would not have been taken away.

I am asking You to forgive them, and for their souls, I mercifully pray. .

Please open their eyes and allow them to see that abortion is not Your will,

So, another life like mine will not be aborted and killed.

When my mother and father had forsaken me, You took me up in Your loving hands.

For they do not know, Lord, that I was created as part of Your divine plan.

I am not speaking to my parents to bring forth guilt and shame.

The enemy is at fault and is the only one to blame.

Abortion is the plot of the enemy to destroy, kill, and steal.

The Lord came to give abundant life that restores and heals.

Lord, please deliver my parents from the sin of abortion today.

I am asking you to forgive them and teach them your righteous ways.

I want to see them one day in the heavens above.

Have mercy upon them with Your unconditional love.

Let the world know that life begins at conception.

That when we repent and humble ourselves, You will offer grace and redemption.

Give my mother and father your precious sight to see,

So, they will not abort another one of God's creation and plan as they have done to me.

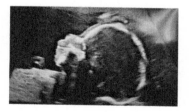

Even if my father and mother abandon me, the LORD will take care of me.

Psalm 27:10 GW

PART TWO

THERE IS HEALING AND FORGIVENESS AFTER ABORTION

God Will Avenge the Stolen Voices

What happened to the life that once grew inside of me?

The life that was growing with my every heartbeat;

No one ever told me that abortion was wrong and against God's will.

That the enemy's evil plan is behind every baby that is killed

I was too young to realize that terminating my pregnancy was not the right option.

I thought it was my only choice to have an abortion.

If I had an ultrasound that revealed the life growing inside my body,

I would not have aborted my baby with her purpose and destiny.

Now I know the Lord's plan is for all babies to live.

They are His gift implanted in the womb that He gracefully gives.

Everything the enemy uses for evil; God will turn around for the good of His perfect will.

Even the aborted babies that mankind daily kills,

They will resurrect one day with the Lord in all His glory.

We will hear their voice as they tell us all their stories.

God will avenge all the babies who cried out to Him day and night.

For He heard their voice that was silenced when abortion took away their birthrights.

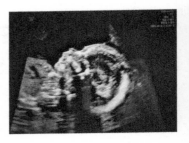

And will not God give justice to his elect, who cry to him day and night? Will he delay long over them?

Luke 18:7 ESV

The Fruit of The Womb

I was lying upon this cold table as I fell into a deep sleep.

For the life growing in my womb, I've convinced myself not to keep.

Fourteen and pregnant, I was left confused and alone.

After I told my boyfriend I was pregnant, he permanently hung up the phone.

I could not find a supportive face in sight,

I had no one to advocate for my baby's birthright.

If someone had told me this would have been my last fruitful day,

Then I would have never made this life-changing decision as I fearfully lay.

There is a part of you that is taken away with abortion.

After the procedure, I had mixed and terrifying emotions.

I bled excessively for the next several days,

I did not know there were retained baby parts hidden and tucked away.

I would have lost my life if I did not go to the hospital in time.

My boyfriend, who said he loved me, I could not locate and find.

After many years, I have decided to marry and moved on with my life,

I finally had the opportunity to become someone's wife,

The family I've always hoped of having would never be.

This vision was taken away when I aborted part of me.

My past caught up with me, and I couldn't tell my husband a lie and live with this deception.

That because of my past abortion, my womb was unable to carry the miracle of conception.

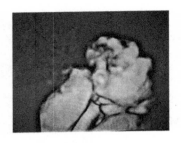

Behold, children are a gift of the LORD,
The fruit of the womb is a reward.

Psalms 127:3 NASB

Be Healed from Abortion My Daughters

Be healed my daughters, from the guilt and shame.

I know after the abortion, you have never been the same.

The pain that you are going through was part of the enemy's plan.

He is the one who tempts and captivates the will of man.

When you aborted the life that was growing inside of your womb,

This opened a door for the enemy to bring you sorrow and doom.

I've instructed man in My Word to be fruitful and multiply.

I AM the Lord who provides and every need I shall supply

The enemy had you believe a lie and has kept you deceived.

Why did you fear? Why have you doubted me?

You may have aborted your baby because it was another mouth to feed.

I have promised never to forsake the righteous and make beggars of their seeds.

I know you are hurting because you have lost a part of you.

Today, I AM offering redemption and my strength to see you through.

I will heal your wombs from the emptiness that lies within.

Take hold of My grace and mercy, for I will no longer remember your sins.

I've sent My Word to heal you from the sins of abortion.

When I clothed you in My righteousness, there is no condemnation.

I AM restoring unto you what the enemy has destroyed and stolen.

I declare reparation for every breach and gap that was broken.

I AM the One who breathes life into the seed that is planted inside the womb of a woman.

Sin no more my daughters, abortion was never part of My divine will and plan.

I am the One who created your babies, they are the work of My hands.

I've come to take away the pain and hurt that you currently feel.

Arise today, my daughters; I declare that you are restored and healed.

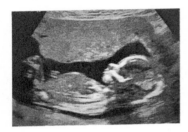

If my people who are called by my name humble themselves and pray and seek my face, and turn from their wicked ways, then I will hear from heaven and will forgive their sin and heal their land.

2 Chronicles 7:14 ESV

I AM Forgiven

I praise you, Lord, for forgiving my past abortion sin.

When I destroyed your precious gifts, I was left so empty within.

The abortions I had so many years ago left me with an empty void.

The Word declares that there is no condemnation for those who are in the Lord.

I've mourned for my babies that one day I will see.

Thank you, Lord, for taking them up when they were rejected by me

Even after you've forgiven me, I continued to feel guilt and shame.

The enemy constantly reminded me of the hurt and pain.

I choose today to overcome the enemy by the word of my testimony.

Whom the Lord has set free, is truly free indeed.

I thank you, Lord, for sending your Word to heal and take me to my expected end.

I decree and declare today that I have been redeemed and forgiven.

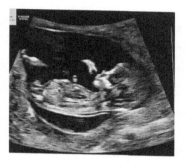

I know the plans that I have for you, declares the LORD. They are plans for peace and not disaster; plans to give you a future filled with hope.

Jeremiah 29:11 GW

I Will Heal Your Womb

Lord, heal my broken heart.

My spirit is torn into pieces from the baby that was ripped apart.

I've aborted my baby with his dreams and destiny.

Now, I'm left with a hole deep inside of me.

This void within was supposed to be filled with my baby's birth.

I never got to see his heartbeat on the ultrasound, and now he's left the earth.

Lord, where do I go from here

For this pain and trauma, I was not prepared.

How do I heal, and who will fill this emptiness embedded deep in my heart?

For I am not able to move like I'm stuck under a heavy rock.

" My precious daughter, I feel your pain and sorrows.

I know I cannot return your gift from the past, but I can promise you tomorrow.

There is healing in My blood that will wash and cleanse your womb.

I will breathe new life in your inner core that was used as your baby's tomb.

I send My Word today to heal your broken heart that will now live for me.

Today, I call you out of your darkness and have set you free.

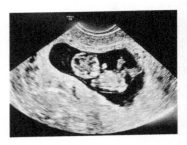

She said in a loud voice, "You are the most blessed of all women, and blessed is the child that you will have.

You are blessed for believing that the Lord would keep his promise to you."

Luke 1:42 & 45

Innocent Blood

Lord, how could anyone hurt these precious little babies?

Mommy and daddy's excuses were that they were not prepared and ready.

Did they not know that poison is injected into their baby's heart?

Would they allow this barbaric act if they saw their baby's limb torn apart?

How could society allow this crime to continue and go on?

Do they not know that abortion kills life and is morally wrong?

Lord, please make the killing of the preborn babies stop.

Please do not let abortion stop another beating heart.

Billions of babies have already been killed,

How much more innocent blood must continue to spill?

Abortion is the silent holocaust of our present day.

Innocent babies are dehumanized, killed, and barbarically slaughtered.

Why can society not see that these are our future sons and daughters?

Lord, please make the killing of these precious babies come to an end.

Their blood is crying out from the ground and waiting to be avenged.

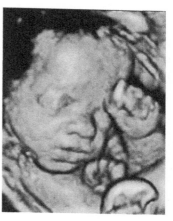

There are six things that the Lord hates, even seven things that are an abomination to him: haughty eyes, a lying tongue, and hands that shed innocent blood,

Proverbs 6:16-17 NET

The Lord Weeps for Our Babies

Sometimes, we hear a cry in our most inward part.

The Spirit of the Lord is calling us deeper to set us apart,

We cry out for the nation that is being destroyed each day.

For the babies that are at risk of dying, we cover and pray.

Mankind is seeking to destroy the marvelous works of your hands.

The wickedness that lies deep in their hearts has become an epidemic in this land.

How can they rip apart babies that are peacefully growing in their mother's womb?

For they did not know what awaited them was an earthly tomb.

Lord, when will the bloodshed stop? Can you hear the baby's' cry?

Mankind is injecting poison into their hearts as they painfully die.

When will they get that abortion is a crime against humanity?

Their minds are corrupted, and hearts are filled with depravity.

These precious babies do not deserve to die,

For you had a good plan for their lives stolen by the enemy's lies.

Lord, you said it in your Word, You hate hands that shed innocent blood.

Raise a standard against the spirit of abortion that has overtaken this nation like a flood.

Lord, have mercy upon this country for its sin has reached an ultimate peak.

We turn our hearts back to You, so Your face we will seek.

Lord, please do not allow mankind to kill one more baby based on their theories and lies.

Expose the hidden deception and darkness so your precious babies will not die.

Lord, lay Your burden for preborn and born-alive babies upon the heart of the Church.

Let us be moved with compassion and love and stop doing unnecessary works.

We drive out complacency from Your Church and apply eye salve upon their eyes.

Lord, expose the sins of abortion and obliterate the enemy's lies.

Lord, I can hear Your Spirit grieving, for the aborted babies, you weep.

Let your tears flood the Church, and Your cry awaken them from their sleep.

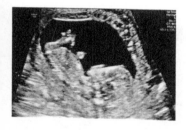

"The king will answer them, 'I can guarantee this truth: Whatever you did for one of my brothers or sisters, no matter how unimportant [they seemed], you did for me.'

Matthew 25:40 GW

We Cry Out for All Babies to Live

Thank you, Lord, for allowing Your precious babies to tell their stories.

One day we will see them all sitting with You in all Your glory.

Mankind has hardened their hearts with their selfish laws that take away the preborn baby's voice.

For they have been silenced, and society keeps aborting them without their consent and choice.

Please overturn Roe, the legislation that steals the preborn baby's birthright.

Raise a standard against the spirit of abortion and put this enemy to flight.

We cry out for all preborn and born babies to be shielded and safe.

Protect these babies from abortion so they will not go to an early grave.

Lord, we overrule the laws of abortion that was written from an ungodly political realm.

We stand in the gap for all preborn and born babies, so abortion will not kill, steal, and destroy them.

I decree that they will walk in the land of the living and see the day of their birth.

I pray that You will give them abundant life, so your purpose they will fulfill upon this earth.

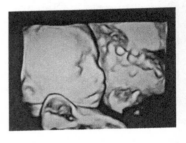

Never give your children as sacrifices to the god Molech [by burning them alive]. If you do, you are dishonoring the name of your God. I am the LORD

Leviticus 18:21 GW

EPILOGUE

This book is an expression of God's heart for the babies in the womb. Every piece was downloaded straight from God's heart. He used my pen to give the voiceless back their identity and personhood.

I am truly blessed and humbled to be chosen by God to fight for the preborn children and to be a support system for women who need to heal from their past abortion regrets.

I can identify with the woman who has had an abortion and the ones who are contemplating one. I was faced with similar dilemmas in my past and unfortunately, I did not choose life for all my children.

I pray that the testimony of my journey from having several abortions and to receive God's healing grace will be a blessing to you. I hope this book helps and guides many who are facing a crisis in pregnancy to choose life for their babies. I also hope that many women will receive healing and deliverance of guilt from their past abortions. I hope that you hear God's still small voice whispering in each of your hearts, telling you that you are forgiven. Be aware that His plans for you are good and not evil.

I praise God that He will use this book to encourage those who are facing a crisis pregnancy to choose life for their precious babies.

I hope you hear the stolen voices in each poetic piece. I hope that you hear the cries for the babies that died in an abortion, those that are presently living in the womb, and those that will be knitted by the Almighty God. Most of all, I hope you hear the cries of your own baby's voice speaking to your heart, saying, "let me live."

A Call to Action

As the Body of Christ, we are instructed to speak for those who cannot speak for themselves. God is calling brave warriors to answer this call.

Who will take a stand and destroy the evil works of the enemy? Who will stand in the gap for the children in the womb?

God's heart is broken, as too many innocent bloods has been shed in this world. The modern-day holocaust, also known as abortion, is real. How could we be sleeping through this when it is happening right before our eyes?

65 million preborn babies have died on American soil and 1.6 billion worldwide. Will we allow future generations to be killed and destroyed by the enemy?

For those that say, "Abortion is not my problem." Abortion will always be our nation's problem if preborn babies are killed in our communities, cities, states, and countries.

Let me tell you how you can help end abortion. Elect those that support abolishing abortion with no exceptions, volunteer or donate to crisis pregnancy centers and advocate for the preborn right to live via social media platform, adopt or become a foster parent, and support women's right to choose life for their babies.

Remember, every life matter in this world; born and preborn. Most of all, they matter to the Almighty God that is sitting upon the throne.

RESOURCES

Even if you have taken the first dose of the abortion pill (Mifeprex or RU-486), you can still save the life of your baby.

Do you regret your decision and wish you could reverse the effects of the abortion pill? There may be help available!

There is an effective process called

abortion pill reversal.

Contact the helpline ASAP. They will talk to you and offer help where necessary.

The helpline will connect you with a medical professional, who will guide you towards reversing the effects of the abortion pill. They will help you every step of the way. Call now!!

CALL THE 24/7 HELPLINE: **(877) 558-0333**

https://abortionpillreversal.com/

My beautiful ladies, please do not listen to anyone that tells you that there is no help available and that abortion is the only option and way out of pregnancy. Once you have an abortion, your baby's life is permanently gone forever. God has made provision for both you and your baby. In this section, you can find the necessary resources that are available that will help make the preparation required to provide for both you and your little one.

PREGNANCY HELP

If you are facing an unplanned pregnancy, looking for an alternative to abortion, or just want to locate the nearest pregnancy resource center (PRC), please call Option Line at 800-712-HELP (800-712-4357). This is a free 24/7 service that can refer you to a PRC in your area where you can get help in person.

You can also text "Helpline" to 313131 or visit OptionLine.org and center.

Care Net – (877) 791-5475 Care Net offers free resources and a confidential, toll-free phone line available from 6 AM to 10 PM ET.

Hidden Choices

Help pregnant teens and women get free resources and the help and support they need.

https://www.hiddenchoices.org

Guiding Star El Paso – (915) 544-9600

Redefining healthcare for women, men, and families, especially during planned or unplanned pregnancy and parenthood. All services are 100% free of charge.

Fiona Jackson Center for Pregnancy

407-533-8680

INFO@FJCENTER.ORG

Pine Hills Location

1336 N. Pine Hills rd.

Orlando, F 32808

West Orange Location

1450 Daniels Rd,

Winter Garden, FL 34787

Woman's New Life Clinic

womansnewlife.com

New Orleans: 504.831.3117

Baton Rouge: 225.663.6470

Pro-Life Resource List

https://www.epm.org/resources/2010/Apr/14/prolife-resource-list/#alternatives

PRO-LIFE Across AMERICA
Hotline: 1-800-366-7773

1st Way Life Center
1-800-848-LOVE (5683)

Total Life Care Clinics
(Minnesota & Wisconsin): 1-888-652-1140 or 651-291-9473

Birthright
1-800-550-4900

First Choice Women's Resource Centers:

www.1stchoice.org

Call: 973-538-0967 or Text 973-532-2904

Marisol Health, a service of Catholic Charities in Denver, is another pro-life service that exists to help pregnant women in need.

https://marisolhealth.com/

Nothing is more stressful than facing financial hardship while navigating an unplanned pregnancy. A branch near you may be able to help with qualified expenses during your pregnancy.

https://impregnant.org/

This organization helps women walking through the unsteady season of an unplanned pregnancy or women navigating single motherhood by connecting them to judgment-free support groups in churches across the world.

https://embracegrace.com/

FOOD

This will help you find help for food;

https://foodstamps.org/

SHELTER

If you are without a place to stay or if you are the victim of violence or abuse and need to get away from the place you are, we have suggested some resources to help you find shelter. If you are being kicked out of your home or forced to get an abortion, there is help and you are not alone.

Contact the nearest *pregnancy resource center* for local recommendations.

Please call **Option Line** at 800-712-HELP (800-712-4357). This is a free 24/7 service that can refer you to a PRC in your area where you can get help in person. You can also text "Helpline" to 313131 or visit OptionLine.org and center.

Local Organizations that provides housing for women and teens who are Pregnant and Homeless.

The Lighthouse for Teen Mothers Housing is for ages 14-19-year-olds, who have chosen life and have chosen to parent.
Go to: lighthouseforteenmoms.org to apply

St Anne's Center, Grandma's House,

A comfortable home for women working toward goals and independence while caring for their little one

(908) 386-2066

www.grandmashouse.us

39 Roseberry St, Phillipsburg,

NJ 08865, US

ADOPTION

The greatest gift you can choose for your baby is life. Many wonderful families are available and are willing to adopt and love your baby as your own.

If you choose adoption as an option, then there are many agencies available in your state of residency.

I have listed a few adoption resources to get you started in the process. Also, you can contact a local pregnancy center and they will help you locate an adoption agency that will help you and your baby

https://lifetimeadoption.com/birthmothers/pregnant-considering-adoption/

Talk about Adoption: Creates awareness about adoption and supports mothers and fathers through their unexpected pregnancy to equip them for parenthood or adoption through one-on-one mentoring.

http://www.talkaboutadoption.org/

Catholic Charities: Offers a directory of country-wide offices to connect you with local counseling, parenting education, and support, adoption assistance.

https://www.catholiccharitiesusa.org/find-help/

Bethany: A global organization that is offering social services designed to help families thrive through essential services, including pregnancy counseling, foster care, emergency care, and adoption.

https://bethany.org/

Lifetime Adoption: Offers comprehensive adoption services, including a 24-hour hotline, counseling, housing, and education about adoption.

SCHOLARSHIPS FOR PREGNANT WOMEN

The website

scholarshipsforwomen.com also lists more than 19 scholarships and grants available to pregnant women of various qualifications. Please take advantage of these opportunities.

Also, take advantage of your local Federal Pell Grants and state grants that will pay for your books and tuition.

Never give up on your goals. If you are in high school, look into childcare programs that will help pay for daycare while you go to school. There is help available. Please do not give up. I took advantage of the government help and resources.

There are additional resources that will help women who are having a difficult time to heal after an abortion. There is help and you do not have to do it alone.

Healing After Abortion

Option Line – (800) 712-4357 | Option Line offers a confidential live chat, text line, and toll-free hotline that is available 24/7. The website contains additional resources for women who are considering abortion, have had an abortion, or are seeking alternatives to abortion.

International Helpline for Abortion Recovery

(866) 482-5433 - Provides confidential care 24/7 for those needing help after an abortion. The helpline is staffed by consultants who have personally experienced the pain of abortion but have also found hope and healing.

Rachel's Vineyard

(877) 467-3463

rachel@rachelsvineyard.org

Rachel's Vineyard offers confidential, weekend programs, and other services across the United States and Canada with additional sites around the world for anyone affected by abortion.

Set Free, Inc.:

Offers a private post-abortive support group, an online healing program, and a yearly healing retreat.

https://setfree-ministry.com/

(203) 631-1065

erikalynn.setfreeministry

Instagram @set_freeministry

Facebook.com/setfreeministry

Project Rachel: Serves anyone suffering from abortion in spiritual and psychological healing, offering tools to express grief and counseling in how to talk to friends and family about your abortion.

Dial 888-456-HOPE (4673) to be connected to a local ministry near you.

https://hopeafterabortion.com/

Shame Free Gigi The Post Abortive Coach

Helps women find post-abortion healing and share their stories.

https://www.youtube.com/c/ShameFreeGigi/featured

ABOUT THE AUTHOR

Nativida Etienne-Maule is a Doctor of Nursing Practice (DNP), who specializes as a Family Nurse Practitioner and believes that all lives should be treated with dignity and respect.

Nativida graduated as a registered nurse in 1999, and due to her passion for providing quality patient care, she obtained her degree as a Family Nurse Practitioner in 2006 at SUNY Downstate Medical Center and obtained her clinical doctorate degree at Old Dominion University in 2013.

Nativida is a visionary and a world changer, who was called by God to destroy the works of the

enemy. She is a licensed minister who answered the call to fight against abortion and help women heal from past trauma.

In 2008, she was called to advocate against abortion after God led her to watch an abortion on the television. It was at that time she felt God's heart for the babies that were killed from abortion's deadly sting. God commissioned her to speak for the babies that had their lives stolen from abortion deadly sting. She speaks for the babies that died, the ones that live, and the ones that will come. Her book "Stolen Voices" is prophetically inspired, life-changing, that is healing many hearts all over the world.

Nativida was ordained and licensed as a minister in the areas of healing and deliverance in 2019. She uses her social media platform to advocate against abortion, reaching millions of people on Instagram @stolen_voices and @stolen_voices_2.

She heard God's heart for the preborn children and their mothers. She heard the call to end

abortion and answered.

She has dedicated her life to be an advocate to end disparities, especially in minority communities, in the areas of abortion, and to help improve healthcare, especially for expectant mothers.

Abortion is the number one killer of black lives in America. She hears the outcry for black women to exit the plantation that was built for them to sacrifice the children in their wombs.

She vows to continue to speak for the children in the wombs, who cannot speak for themselves until abortion is abolished and becomes unthinkable.